DRAWING BUILDINGS

Companion Volumes
ANATOMY AND LIFE DRAWING
DRAWING ANIMALS AND BIRDS
DRAWING BOATS AND WATER
Don Davy

DRAWING BUILDINGS

DON DAVY

A PENTALIC BOOK

TAPLINGER PUBLISHING COMPANY

NEW YORK

First published in the United States in 1981 by
TAPLINGER PUBLISHING CO., INC.
New York, New York

Copyright © 1981 Blandford Press Ltd,
Link House, West Street,
Poole, Dorset BH15 1LL

Library of Congress Catalog Card Number: 81–50606
ISBN 0–8008–2267–6

Contents

Acknowledgements

The author would like to express his gratitude to the following people for the help he has received in compiling this book:

Sylvia Davy, Leatherhead
Mr & Mrs A. Bullen, Swanworth Farm
Joy Real, Witley
Frank Stokes, Lloyds Bank, Leatherhead
Philip Spencer, Norbury Park House
Bill Voss, Ashford, Middlesex
Mike Nevins, Dorking

Paul Cosway, Sunbury-on-Thames
Geoffrey Dakin, Ashford, Middlesex
Celia Featherstone, Sydney, Australia
Sonia Kennerley, Crundale, Kent
Staff of Leatherhead Library
Staff of Staines Library

Opening Illustrations:
p. i Carved horse head in English stableyard.
p. ii Entrance, Norbury Park House, Surrey.
p. iv Carved Greek Capital.

p. v Cornish Tin Mine.
p. vi Village Pump, Ockley, Surrey.

TO THE TILLINGBOURNE PEOPLE

Men and words are actual and you painter, if you do not know how to execute your figures, will be like an orator who does not know how to use his words.
The painter who knows by practice and judgement of eye without the use of reason, is like the mirror which reproduces within itself all the objects opposite to it without knowledge of the same.

Leonardo da Vinci

Tillingbourne House, Wotton, Surrey, England.

Introduction

Buildings, from the earliest mud hut to the finest palace, have always been of the greatest importance to man. Primarily as places to provide shelter and warmth from the elements, they were gradually improved until they became places of security and pleasure for ourselves and our possessions. They can be things of beauty or ugliness, depending on the prevailing fashion or whim of the builder or owner, and on the availability of materials.

As artists we have to consider how to illustrate buildings in the best possible way to obtain the maximum effect from our pictures. To achieve this a basic study of perspective and light and shade is necessary, as well as techniques suitable to the particular subject.

We all have our favourite subject. Always among the most popular are the thatched cottage, and the half timbered house or inn. (Christmas cards reflect this popularity.) Buildings which feature greatly in art books are churches and cathedrals of all kinds. But whatever the structures we wish to portray in our pictures it is important to give them the correct setting and to make them look solid and authentic; this is where perspective, light and shade and proportion are so useful.

A by-product of the study of buildings is learning to observe more readily many of the details which we normally take for granted and, indeed, some of which we may never have seen at all. Unless we specifically go to visit a particular building, we do not usually see all the richness around us. How many of us know what the upper stories above our local supermarket are like? Are there any windows and gables? Is there brickwork or cement facing? Are there any embellishments? It is worth having a good look the next time we are in the High Street.

The surroundings of buildings are also very significant, such as trees and foliage, pavements and street lamps, signs, etc., as they form an essential part of the complete environment.

It is attention to detail which makes the study of buildings so fascinating. For this reason the subject is to be recommended for artists — it will at the same time have the effect of making us more aware of our heritage.

Glamis Castle, Angus, Scotland.

Basic Construction

Buildings in their simplest form are merely a series of geometric shapes: cubes and cones, spheres interlaced with squares, oblongs, triangles and circles. As they are solid objects we have to express them by obeying the rules of perspective (pages 11–13).

The easiest drawing to be made of any building is the flat elevation because little or no perspective is involved. By using a very simple and direct technique such a drawing can be very attractive. As long as the proportion and dimensions are correct, it is merely a case of putting all the details in the right places and the drawing emerges. Such a drawing rarely shows any real solidity; it has the appearance of a flat illustration or diagram, rather than having a three dimensional interest which is created by using perspective to supply the illusion of depth.

Phillips House, Dinton, Wiltshire, England.

By using an angled view point, a feeling of 'going into the picture' is created as well as the sense that one expects to know what is around the sides of the building. In this way there begins to be a completeness, a solidity.

The building selected to be drawn should be stripped in the mind's eye of all its trappings of detail and decoration. It is then reduced to its basic form which is sometimes merely a simple box surmounted by a prism shape. Having established these simple shapes in the correct perspective, all the details may then be applied. There is nothing more annoying than to spend an enormous amount of time on a detailed drawing only to find that the basic shape, or perspective, is wrong and the whole picture is ruined.

Westwood Manor, Wiltshire, England.

Perspective

It is necessary to have a simple working knowledge of perspective to make our drawings of buildings appear solid and convincing. If we remember that most things can be reduced to boxes this exercise should present few difficulties.

The horizon, or eye-line, is the first thing to consider. Wherever you are placed in relation to your subject is the determining factor in establishing your perspective. Let us take this one step at a time. To find the horizon line you want you must consider how you wish to portray your subject matter. Fig. 1 illustrates the normal view one has of a building, i.e. where the eye is level with the doorway, about 5' 6" from the ground.

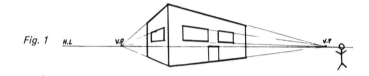

Fig. 1   H.L   V.P   V.P

Now if it is desired to make a building appear bigger and grander, it is necessary to lower one's eye-line to ground level for a worm's eye view.

In Fig. 2, the artist is lying on the ground with the building towering above.

Fig. 2   H.L   V.P   V.P

The final aspect to remember is where the subject can be made to look small, similar to a doll's house, by raising the eye high in the sky above the subject. Fig. 3 illustrates how this is done.

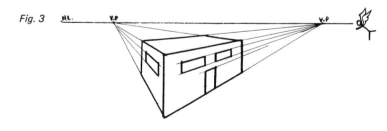

Fig. 3   H.L.   V.P   V.P

Having established where we want our eye-line, it is time to find out how to put the simple rules of perspective into practice. Here we are dealing mainly with parallel perspective, which means that lines parallel to each other converge on the same vanishing point. To understand what a vanishing point is, look at Fig. 4 and imagine that you are standing on a desert with a straight road disappearing to the horizon. Although we know that the two lines of the road edges are the same width all the way along, the appearance is that they go away from us and converge at one point, vanishing on the horizon. Parallel lines always vanish to one point on the horizon.

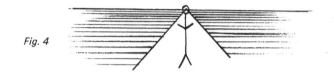

Fig. 4

Let us see what this concept looks like when it is applied to a box-like structure. Fig. 5 shows two sides of a box with the eye-line established in the middle. Each side has two parallel lines and therefore two vanishing points. The placing of the vanishing points is a matter of practice, but it should be remembered that the more one can see of the side of a building the further the vanishing point is from the leading edge, and conversely the less seen of the side of the building the nearer the vanishing point is to the leading edge.

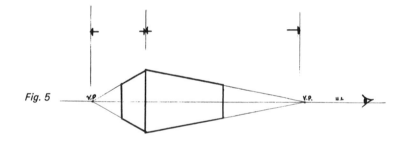

Fig. 5

For all practical purposes the vertical lines are placed where appropriate and kept absolutely vertical.

Let us work out how to put a roof on to our box-like building. To find the apex of the roof, we must first of all find the main lines of the hidden part of the building. Fig. 6 shows us how this is achieved. Fig. 5 is drawn again, then the hidden lines are drawn, following the rule that parallel lines must disappear to the same vanishing points. The appearance of our drawing is now that of a glass box.

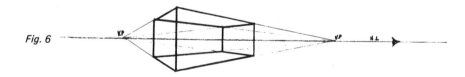

Fig. 6

We now have to find the centre of the side of the building where we wish to project the gable end. This is very simply done by drawing two diagonal lines from corner to corner, which gives us a centre point; then we can project a vertical line through this, see Fig. 7. Somewhere along this line the apex point of the roof is fixed.

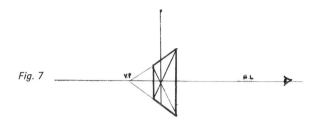

Fig. 7

A line is then drawn from the apex point to the appropriate vanishing point. See Fig. 8.

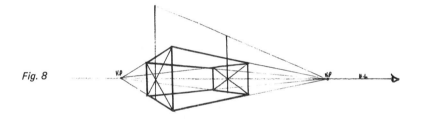

Fig. 8

Now all we have to do is to join up the points from the apex to the edges of the roof and we have a simple building cube with a roof. See Fig. 9.

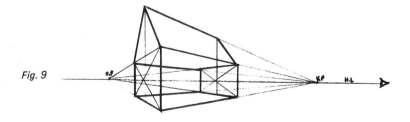

Fig. 9

Light and Shade

The gradual building up of your picture now takes on another dimension, that of light and shade. Using strong light and a carefully chosen angle, the building being drawn can be made to look very solid by making one of its planes darker than the other. The use of very dark areas on a building can also add an element of drama to your drawing.

The use of this technique is obviously more effective when drawing older or more complicated buildings, simply because there are more bits and pieces to cast shadows. It will be seen on this page that the drawing of the old barn relies heavily on the shadows cast by the timber planking as well as the broad light and dark areas on the building itself.

On the following pages the effect of bright light and heavy shadows is obvious. It will be noted that the darker the shadow the brighter the lighter parts appear. Using carved figures on a building adds a bonus to this effect, particularly where drapery and carved woodwork are concerned. The drawing of The Jew's House, Lincoln, illustrates the interesting effects which can be achieved by the introduction of heavy shadows underneath the stonework on the surface of the building. Even if, when drawing your subject, the prevailing light is not very intense, you can translate it to make it look so by picking out the broad aspects first and then identifying all the details.

Old Barn, Swanworth Farm, Surrey, England.

Abinger Hammer,
Surrey, England.

Caryatids, Erechtheum, Athens.

Bracket,
Indian Temple.

The Great Wall of China.

15

The Jew's House, Lincoln, England.

Stratford-upon-Avon, Warwickshire, England.

Special Techniques

There are many varied ways of depicting all kinds of textures which we find on buildings. The variation on a theme is as complex as the buildings themselves. Throughout this book there are hundreds of different examples, but a few of the most common are selected on page 18. These are examples of what to look for. As a general rule of thumb I usually try to 'feel' the texture and draw accordingly, e.g. glass, I use hard and sharp pencil strokes (note the example on this page), not only are there clearly defined areas of reflection, either dead black or shades of grey, but skirting around the engraved decoration on the glass itself. There are also ceramic tiles comprising the whole surface of the building which are also dealt with in a similar crisp fashion. Overleaf it will be seen that great use is made of dark shadows to delineate the pieces of stone, tiles and some wooden structures, but in the case of brickwork the bricks themselves are accented rather than the spaces between.

Many of the techniques usually depend upon how you, the artist, see the structure and texture. It can be said that brick and stone are hard materials, but it may be that the surface is soft in texture and should be treated as such, but on the other hand it is difficult to suggest that glass or ceramic tiles are soft, so it may be easier to decide that a hard approach is necessary. The best method always is to practise and try out many techniques to prove to yourself the right approach for you.

Rea's Bar, Aberystwyth, Wales.

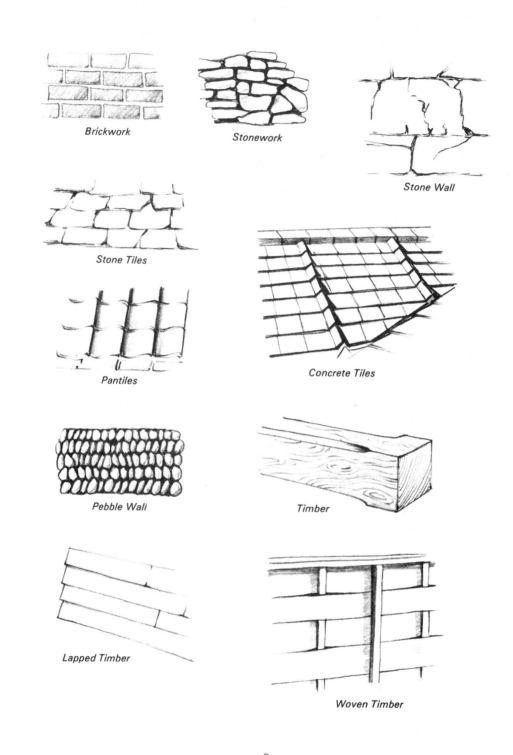

Brickwork

Stonework

Stone Wall

Stone Tiles

Concrete Tiles

Pantiles

Pebble Wall

Timber

Lapped Timber

Woven Timber

18

The Town Hall, Croydon, Surrey, England.

Choice of Subjects

It is overwhelming when one considers the fantastic choice open to us. Everything from a garden shed to a palace, a cottage to a cathedral. We all have our preferences and in a sense this limits our selections; it could also be said that our expertise may determine what we draw. Whatever we choose for our subject, we should never be put off by the apparent complexity; until we try we do not have any idea of our capacity. It is good to make mistakes, it is possibly the quickest way to learn. Once having identified a problem it is up to us to isolate it and practise until it is solved.

There are many tricks to be mastered, not the least being the surroundings to our buildings, i.e. water, trees, skies, etc., etc. – the list can be almost inexhaustible. Do not forget that whatever you are drawing basic rules apply, those of light, shade, perspective and composition.

Whatever you choose to draw, try to make it something which really interests and fascinates you. It is much better to be spurred on by 'wanting' to draw than just making a boring exercise. Do try to enjoy every drawing you do, the result will be so much better.

St Irene, Istanbul, Turkey.

Outwood Mill, Surrey, England.

Donaghadee Harbour Lighthouse, Co. Down, Ireland.

Cormac's Chapel, Tipperary, Ireland.

Cob Cottages, Minehead, Somerset, England.

22

Choice of Setting

There are so many venues in which our buildings can be illustrated that it is difficult sometimes to make a choice. The first thing to consider is the setting in which the chosen subject actually is. Question whether it is exactly as you want it. Consider whether the drawing you are doing is to be a faithful representation of the scene – a true record – or to be a picture to be made more acceptable in composition by taking a few liberties with the placing, or by removing certain objects around the building.

If the picture is for us alone it must be remembered that we dictate the scene – not the scene us – as we are the masters of the picture, not the other way round.

Cragside, Northumberland, England.

Old Sussex Barn, England.

Crofter's Cottage, Isle of Skye, Scotland.

Thatched Cottages, Luccombe, Somerset, England.

25

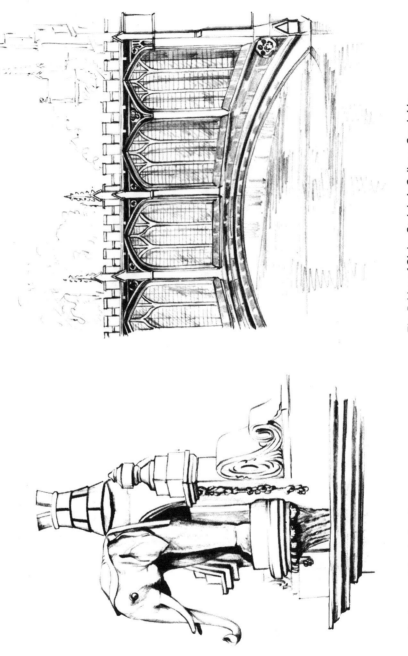

The Bridge of Sighs, St John's College, Cambridge.

Elephant and Castle, London.

26

Planning Your Picture

The first thing to consider, having chosen the subject, is what the best viewpoint is and where on the paper the main subject shall be placed. Next, we begin to observe a few rules of composition. It must be remembered that it is as well to know a few simple rules if only for the reason that we may find it necessary to break them occasionally. It is always better to deviate from established practice from knowledge, rather than to achieve a result by accident and not know how it was done.

It is logical to work out the best way to illustrate the subject in such a way as to enhance the central theme of the picture. Having worked out the central aspect, the technical perspective angle, as well as light and shade, one can start by drawing some thumb-nail sketches to prove to oneself that the composition will work.

page 29

page 46

page 28

page 41

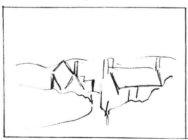

page 42

page 43

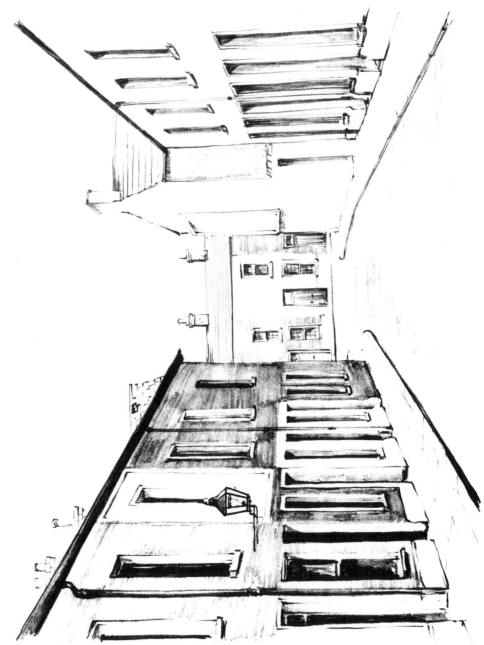

Artisans' Houses, Belfast, Northern Ireland.

28

Hypostyle Hall, Karnak, Egypt.

Buildings Old and New

All over the world there is a wealth of buildings, new and old. Depending on the type of pictures you wish to draw, there is no lack of reference wherever you care to look. Many popular pictures portray old buildings for obvious evocative reasons. There is a nostalgic and romantic longing, perhaps in many of us, for the little thatched cottage with roses round the door 'away from it all', or for the spacious proportions of the Georgian villa – in fact something to which we can relate in scale and style. Apart from these reasons, there is also a case for visual record of famous buildings such as palaces and great houses.

There are many people who find excitement in drawing the buildings in large industrial complexes which can give a great amount of scope in pure line and design.

Whatever the subject, large or small, the basic rules apply. The choice to the artist is really one of technique. On the next few pages there is a selection of examples, but there are many more in the rest of the book.

Home of Louisa May Alcott, Concord, Mass., USA.

Moreton Hall, Cheshire, England.

Modern House, Essex, England.

A Cleitt, St Kilda, Western Isles, Scotland.

Kinwarton Dovecote, Warwickshire, England.

The Tower of London.

Science Lecture Room, Oxford University, England.

Stonehenge, England.

33

Lord Leycester's Hospital, Warwick, England.

Le Corbusier's Villa Savoye, Poissy, France.

Houghton Mill, Huntingdonshire, England.

Sandhopper.

Liberian Mud Hut.

The Oast House, Staines, England.

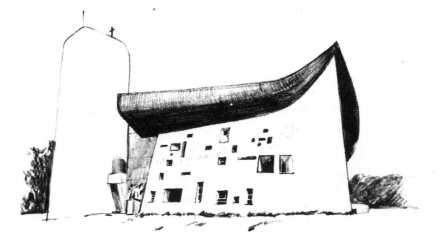

Notre Dame du Haut, Ronchamp, France.

Cottages and Crofts

Cottages and crofts are perhaps among the most popular subjects for picture-making. They are very appealing in themselves but the materials involved – thatch, old bricks and stone, timber and tiles, all with their different textures – give the artist an opportunity to try out a great range of techniques.

In other sections of this book there are methods shown of how to approach the many different surfaces which go to make up attractive pictures. If one includes the varied textures of trees and shrubs, fences, stone walls and all the other paraphernalia set into a good composition, there is no reason why good pictures cannot be made.

It must be stressed that drawing from the real thing in the sketch book gives the authenticity required. Using the pencil and sketch book as an automatic extension of the eye, brain and hand is therefore to be highly recommended.

Burton Bradstock, Dorset, England.

Swanworth Farm, Leatherhead, Surrey, England.

Period Cottages, Shere, Surrey, England.

Preston Mill, East Linton, Scotland.

The Old Post Office, Tintagel, Cornwall, England.

Log Farm House, Great Smoky Mountains, USA.

Swanworth Farm, Leatherhead, Surrey, England.

Crofters' Cottages, Scotland.

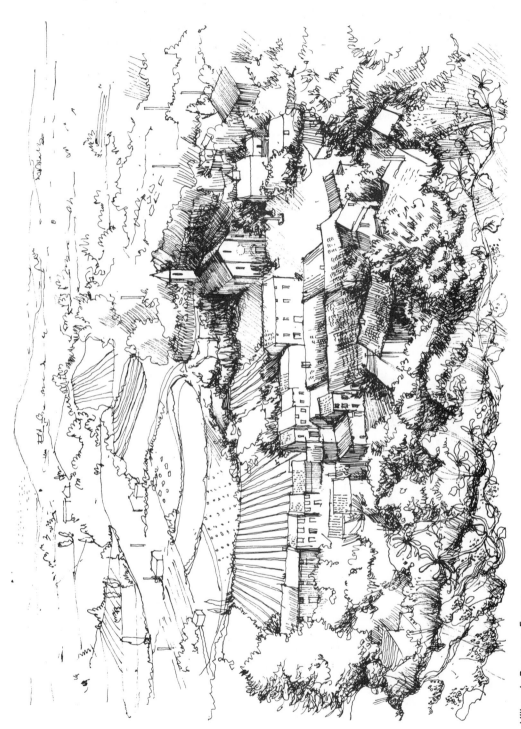

Village in Provence, France.

Churches and Cathedrals

After cottages and rural subjects, churches and cathedrals are probably some of the most popular buildings for drawing. The simple country church is easier to start with. These are usually large box-like shapes, with the addition of, perhaps, a spire which sometimes has a decorative surface of stone or flint. In its churchyard setting with trees, bushes and gravestones the picture is almost ready made.

One must not, however, be daunted by the more massive and apparently complex cathedral. The basic shape is still there and remembering one's perspective the eye-line appears lower because much of the structure is above you. This gives added height and grandeur.

Detail from Southwell Minster, England.

On top of the basic structure are then added all the bits and pieces such as buttresses, windows, battlements, columns, domes and spires which, when combined, enshrine the magnificence of such buildings. One must look for the order amongst this apparent jumble of masonry and it is worth a little time to look at it and sort it out carefully. Pages 46 and 49 are excellent examples of two different view points and two differing techniques, one being a pen and ink drawing which stresses the vertical lines of the building, while the other in pencil shows a softer perspective angle with an emphasis on light and shade.

Some of the interior features are worth drawing for the pure fun of it.

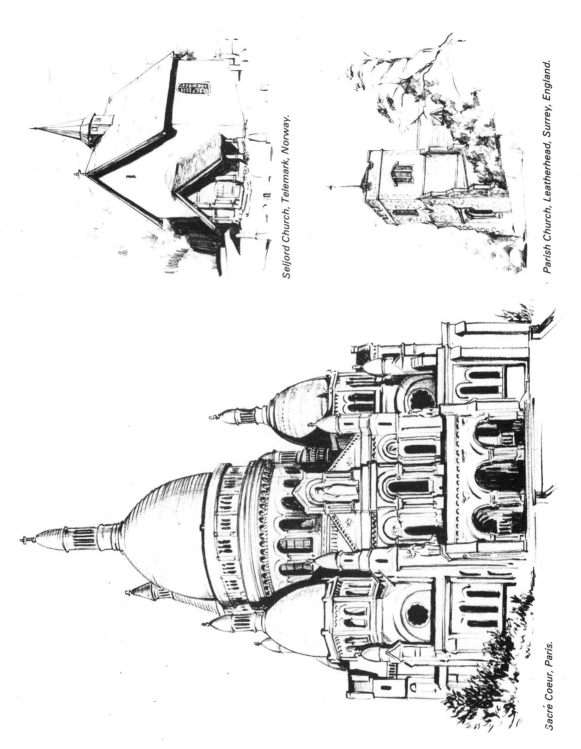

Seljord Church, Telemark, Norway.

Parish Church, Leatherhead, Surrey, England.

Sacré Coeur, Paris.

45

York Minster, England.

Austrian Mountain Church.

Wren's Dial, Oxford, England.

The Acropolis, Athens.

St Bride's Church, London.

Exeter Cathedral, England.

St Mary-le-Bow, London.

48

Lincoln Cathedral, England.

St Patrick's Church of Ireland Cathedral, Armagh.

Carvings from Exeter Cathedral, England.

Palaces and Great Houses

Palaces and great houses embody, with cathedrals and churches, much of the richness of the world's architecture and also reflect the inventiveness and ingenuity of man throughout his historic progress. The difficulty in dealing with these types of buildings is to know what to choose and where to start.

It has always been my practice to carry my sketch book and to be ready and prepared when opportunities arise. It is not a daily occurrence for most of us to be in the presence of a palace or house of historic interest. When on holiday, there are ample opportunities to visit stately

Powis Castle, Wales.

No. 10 Downing Street, London.

homes and usually one can spend a pleasant day drawing and looking. Although it is possible to draw from photographs, and this is an excellent way to practise, there is nothing like drawing from the real thing, choosing your own view and drinking in the atmosphere created around such magnificent structures.

Whatever the type of building and however complicated it may at first appear, do not panic, but remember the stages already stated of looking for the basic form first, getting your perspective right, and adding all the decorative paraphernalia later.

51

Brighton Pavilion, England.

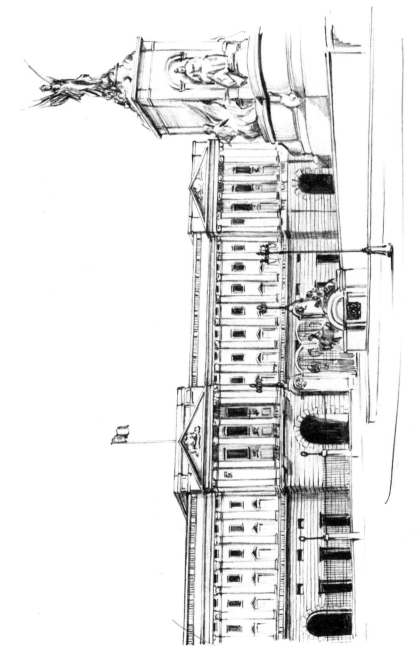

Buckingham Palace, London.

Chatsworth, England.

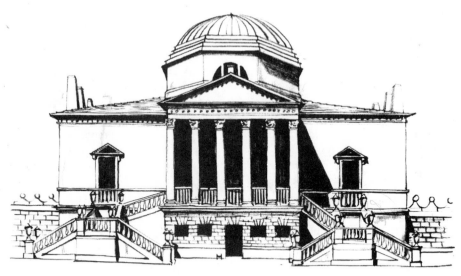

Chiswick House, London, England.

Giffords Hall, Suffolk, England.

Suburbia

It may seem extraordinary at first to think of even considering the subject of suburbia for the artist's attention. One generally equates the suburbs with rows of boring semi-detached houses repeating themselves for mile upon mile, but a closer look reveals all sorts of interesting variations worthy of our notice.

Even when confronted with rows of identical houses, from certain view points the very repetitiveness gives quite an exciting design and pattern which may appeal to some. As many of us live in semi-detached houses there may also be a case for making a picture as a record, which can be far more attractive than a photograph.

One can find many varied styles of architecture in our suburbs which have been handed down to us since the time of the Industrial Revolution and the subsequent exodus from the towns and cities to the outskirts where clean air could be enjoyed. Most of the planning was haphazard, and peculiar pockets of old architecture can be found crammed by the ever-present developer into the spaces left.

There are old and modern examples, whether it be the well-known types of houses included in the ribbon development outside our cities, or the well-planned suburb. So the subject is worth a great deal of study and we certainly should not dismiss that which is, for many of us, right on our doorstep. In many cases we need only to sit in our front parlours to start drawing.

Typical Semi-detached Houses, England.

Garden Suburb, Letchworth, England.

Semi-detached House, New Malden, England.

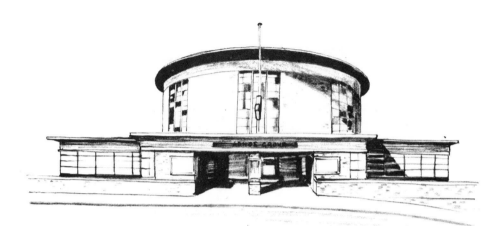

Arnos Grove Underground Station, London.

Modern Flats, Amersham, Buckinghamshire, England.

Lloyds Bank, Leatherhead, Surrey, England.

59

Skyscrapers

The most important thing to remember about drawing tall buildings is the perspective angle. By the very nature of the subject, one is generally near the base of the building and the aspect is therefore of it towering above you. The illustration on this page of the Post Office Tower, London, is especially interesting as it is based on a series of circles in perspective. Starting with a straight line at the bottom (the eye-line), all the circles from there on gradually become more recognisable ellipses (see diagram).

On a further page the drawing of the Seagram Building, New York, has a different point of view. The eye-line is set half-way up the building and, although it is tall, such a view point does not give quite the enormous grandeur that a low eye-line can give. The buildings in Brasilia are treated in rather a geometric fashion, which is just another approach to picture-making and again the eye-line is low.

The drawing of the Manhattan skyline is a superb illustration of a magnificent pattern, found nowhere else in the world, which typifies this type of drawing. A great mass of skyscrapers forming a cement and glass forest of buildings is treated very simply but effectively.

One must never be put off by the apparent complexity of the subject. Again, the basic boxes are inherent, except that there are many of them, but once your perspective is settled in your mind, all there is to do is to draw all the boxes with the attendant light and shade.

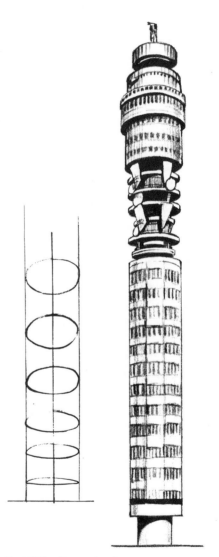

Post Office Tower, London.

60

New York Skyline.

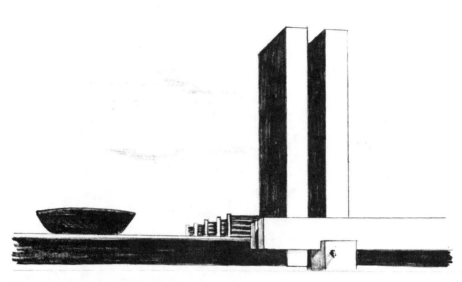

Niemeyer's Buildings, Brasilia, Brazil.

Seagram Building, New York.

Sagrada Familia, Barcelona.

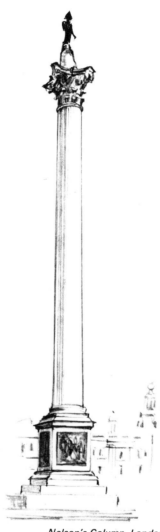

Nelson's Column, London.

63

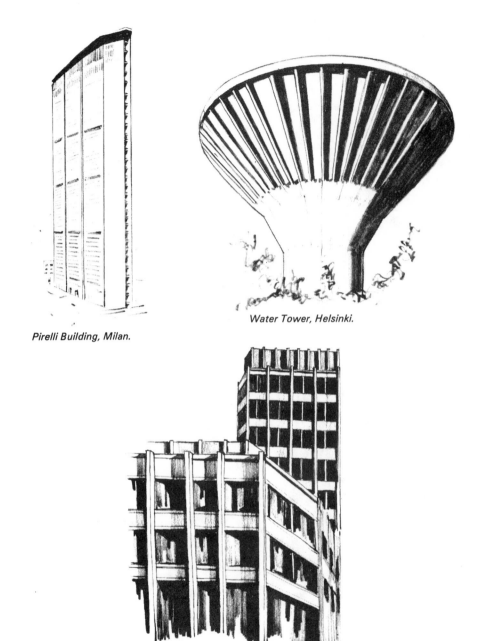

Pirelli Building, Milan.

Water Tower, Helsinki.

The Economist Building, London.

Sheds and Greenhouses

It may seem at first that sheds and greenhouses are hardly worthy of the artist's consideration, but it is worth taking a second look because the challenge presented in drawing them is fun, and the results can be very attractive.

In the section on special techniques there is a reference to drawing glass which is very relevant in the case of greenhouses. When drawing sheds, the details concerning timber should be of great help.

The illustrations give some idea of the range available. Sheds can be the tiny constructions one sees on almost any allotment, the slightly more sophisticated garden shed, or larger buildings which may be chicken houses or farm equipment sheds. With greenhouses the scope is similarly varied, ranging from cold frame and garden greenhouse to the great glass and palm houses in botanical gardens.

The application may not be very obvious at first but if your picture happens to include a garden, it is quite possible that any of the smaller items mentioned could feature, and it is just as well to consider how to draw them properly.

Remember that the same rules apply as if you were drawing a large building. First the basic shape, the perspective angle, the light and shade, and then the applicable techniques.

Garden Greenhouse.　　　　　　　　*Allotment Shed.*

The Great Palm House, Kew Gardens, England.

*Conservatory, Alton Towers,
Staffordshire, England.*

*Conservatory, Norbury Park House,
Surrey, England.*

Conservatory, Montacute House, Yeovil, England.

Cold Frames.

Lean-to Greenhouse.

Castles and Follies

I could not resist including here a drawing of what in my opinion is probably the most marvellous folly of all time – Disneyland. Most follies were built by wealthy gentry to express a whim, or to create some amusement, and this was usually enjoyed by the privileged few. But Disneyland has been and will be enjoyed by many hundreds of thousands of people and this adventure into architectural fantasy is one of the aspects of this great show. If one ever wanted to draw a fairy castle, one need look no further.

Although this section is devoted to castles, there are of course many other examples in this book, but in the ones I have chosen I have tried to depict various methods of approach already suggested. Above all, the approach for me is always suggested by the subject itself.

Disneyland, USA.

Château de Maintenon, France.

Kidwelly Castle, South Wales.

Edinburgh Castle, Scotland.

Bodiam Castle, Sussex, England.

Windsor Castle, England.

Interiors and Ornament

The interiors of buildings are as varied as the outsides. As for ornament, the range of examples is almost limitless. The examples on this page show the fun that can be enjoyed by choosing timbers and stones for their textures, and on subsequent pages the rough surfaces of the brickwork of the Tudor rural interior can be compared with the sleek clean lines of the modern.

Ornament, as mentioned in previous chapters, is a great asset to any drawing in creating extra interest; it can be quiet and discreet as in the balustrade illustration, or overdone and wildly

The Great Barn, East Riddlesden Hall, Yorkshire, England.

exuberant as in the drawing of the museum entrance in Valencia. It is possible that one will enjoy drawing such subjects just for pure fun, but the gentle reminder should be given that even if one is drawing for mere amusement in order to get the most out of it, attention should be paid to the basics of perspective and light and shade.

It is worth looking at the many drawings in this book to study the many different ways of depicting ornament. Some ornament you will notice is just quietly added to the building while in other cases it makes a very important feature.

The Keep Hall, Bamburgh Castle, Northumberland, England.

Tudor Rural.

Renaissance.

Modern.

Modern.

Wall Fountain, Bramham Park,
Yorkshire, England.

Museum Entrance, Valencia, Spain.

Sanctuary Knocker,
Durham Cathedral,
England.

Balustrade at Charlecote, Stratford,
England.

73

Buildings of the World

As I have said before, we are very lucky to have millions of buildings to draw from all over the world; we can never hope to exhaust our stock of reference. On our own doorsteps there are examples on which to practise. We can visit stately homes and palaces, cottages, crofts and seaside buildings when on holiday. There are our well-stocked libraries for thousands of photographs, if we are not lucky enough to go abroad to draw from the real thing in other countries.

There is no excuse for denying ourselves the pleasure of drawing what we want, whenever we want, in this day and age; there is always some source of reference if we only take the trouble to look for it. On these last pages I have tried to show a few subjects throughout the world for which visual references are readily available, either through the local libraries from reference books, other books and magazines, or from photographs taken on holidays and day trips, as well as drawings done with the ever-present sketch book.

All the techniques I have suggested are contained in these drawings which are relevant to the subjects chosen. One can sit down during a winter evening and practise from photographs in the comfort of your own home and thereby gather the skill and the courage necessary to go forth in the fine weather to draw from life with confidence.

Turfed Roofed Barns, Oslo.

74

Ponte Vecchio, Florence.

The Opera House, Sydney, NSW.

Santa Sophia, Turkey.

The White House, Washington.

Pagoda, Japan.

Minaret,
Isfahan, Iran.

St Basil, Moscow.

Taj Mahal, India.

Elephant Gate, Carlsberg Brewery, Denmark.

The Leaning Tower of Pisa.

Doorway, Florence.

Temple of Quetzaleatl, Mexico.

Fantoft Stave Church, near Bergen, Norway.

Copenhagen Stock Exchange, Denmark.

Shrine, Malaga, Spain.

Arsenal Tower, Amsterdam.

Notre Dame, Paris.

St Michael's Mount, Cornwall, England.

79

Mud Houses, Mali.

Yam House, Trobriand Islands.

Riverside Dwelling, Thailand.

Polperro, Cornwall, England.

Neuschwanstein Castle, Bavaria.

Greek Church.

St Paul's Cathedral, London.

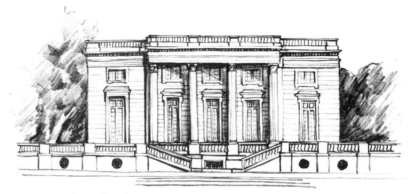

Petit Trianon, Versailles, France.

Temple of Rameses II, Egypt.

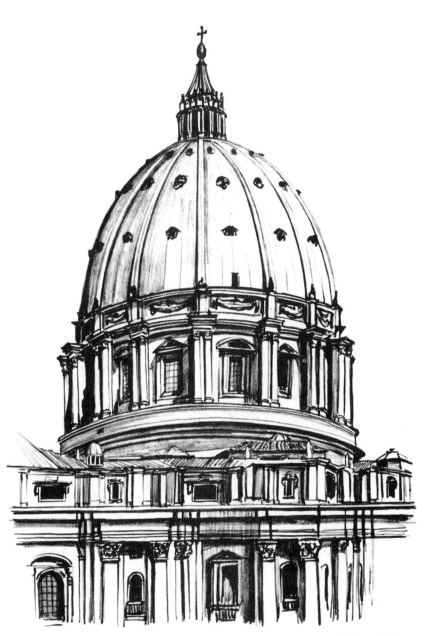

St Peter's, Rome.

85

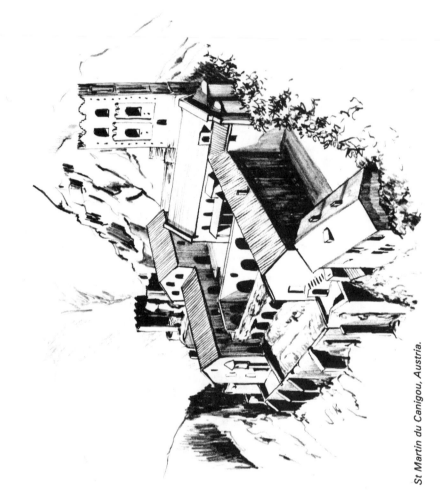

St Martin du Canigou, Austria.

Arc de Triomphe, Paris.

St James's Palace, London.

Arch of Titus, Rome.

*'Falling Water', Bear Run, Pennsylvania, USA,
designed by Frank Lloyd Wright.*

Palace of Knossos, Crete.

Epidaurus Theatre, Greece.

Capitol, Washington, DC.

The Governor's House, Williamsburg, USA.

Pargetting Work, Ipswich, England.

93

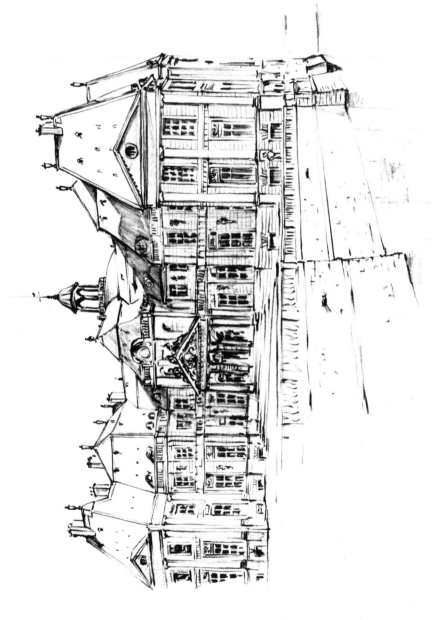

Palace of Versailles, France.

Hardwick Hall, England.

Conclusion

What have we achieved at the end of this book? I have tried to lead the reader gently through the basics of drawing buildings, to choose the subjects and settings to make good pictures, to study the various ways that textures and techniques can be used to make our buildings look authentic. I have also indicated where to find the subjects we wish to portray.

All there is to do now is to practise. I'm afraid that there is no short cut but to draw and draw, again and again, until a satisfactory result is achieved. But, make no mistake, the joy and benefits you will receive will be incalculable. Finally, do remember that you have a talent which is a sin to ignore; it will only grow and develop if it is exercised and tended. It is a privilege to have been granted such a talent, never let it go to waste.

Pillars and capitals, the Forum, Rome.